My Sword, My Tongue

Debra J. Bettis Holt

Unless otherwise noted, all scripture taken
from the King James Version of The Holy Bible.

Copyright © 2017 Debra J. Bettis Holt
All rights reserved

ISBN-10: 1-946106-20-8
ISBN-13: 978-1-946106-20-9

Published by:
Glorified Publishing
PO Box 8004
The Woodlands, TX 77387
www.GlorifiedPublishing.com

Printed in the USA

Megan Holt, Editor
James Nesbit, Cover Image
Abigail Holt-Allen, Author Photograph

DEDICATION

This Book is Dedicated to my Husband David Holt whom I have loved and been married to for thirty-nine years. He has loved me when the Sword in my mouth has brought great glory and when it has brought great pain. He has journeyed with me through many trials and triumphs. Thank You for all the blessings.

CONTENTS

	Acknowledgments	i
1	My Sword, My Tongue Brings Life	1
2	My Sword, My Provision	5
3	My Sword Carves My Relationships	9
4	My Sword, My Tongue of Reproof	13
5	My Sword in the Sheath	15
6	My Sword, My Tongue of Obedience	19
7	My Sword, His Reward	23
8	My Sword, The Harvest Sickle	25
	About the Author	29

My Sword, My Tongue

Debra J. Bettis Holt

ACKNOWLEDGMENTS

I would like to acknowledge my Family for their times of Faithfulness firstly and for their acts of service to the Kingdom of God along side me.

My Mother was the first to tell me of Jesus! Also there are many Spiritual Mentors that have transferred light and love to me along the way:
> Pastors Doug and Rosemary Lowery
> Carol Jontry
> Anita Mason
> John Harper
> Edie Bayer
> Rick Claeson
> Kay Hill
> Kenny and Linda Hinkle

.The Body of Christ is a beautiful thing. We all need each other to survive.

My Sword, My Tongue

1. MY SWORD, MY TONGUE BRINGS LIFE

Beautiful things happen at the command of Our sword, Our tongue, when used at the prompting of God's Love! I have seen broken hearts mended, lives restored, legs grown to the proper length, and addicts set free... all at the use of God's Word across lips.

One story that comes to mind recently was a young mother probably in her mid-twenties whom doctors and surgeons had told she was hopelessly forced to live in back pain the rest of her life due to scoliosis.

We women were sitting around a table at Life Streams Center in Decatur at a prayer meeting. I looked at a seasoned Intercessor friend next to me. We looked at each other at the same time and the same non-acceptance of this diagnosis rose up in us. I boldly spoke out, "Oh Heck No! That is not God's will for you!" We all gathered and laid hands on her and began to thank God that he loved her and that He still is the Healer!

In faith I thanked him that He is the healer and at that very moment her body began to shift and contort a bit. Then, her leg grew out ¾ of an inch! She was healed! God didn't even wait for me to use the rest of my fancy words for the request. He did it before I even commanded it to be healed! Imagine, on his own time schedule!

What's even funnier is that the night before I had been given a Word. I heard in the night, "Let the healings begin." I said, "Ok, Lord but you're going to have to show me what that looks like." Well, He sure did… the next day.

Use your tongue for the supernatural. When the Holy Spirit rises up in you that something is not right- or not His will… just say no! Let the sword of faith in God and His Word be on fire on your tongue!

Release with the sword of the Lord the desire of heaven. His word and His will on your tongue. We hear often that we are His hands and His feet. I say, "Lets be His mouth, His sword!" There is Life or Death in the power of the tongue the Bible says.

The same seasoned intercessor that was with me for the healed leg said to me once, "God's Word in your mouth has the same effect as God's Word in His mouth. You are his ambassador."

One of the giants in the Army of God taught me a powerful concept: Carol Jontry is one of the most powerful Intercessors I've ever met. I have said of her on more than one occasion, "When Carol's feet hit the floor in the morning- the devil says, "Oh No! Carol's awake!" The enemy trembles at a Christian with their sword aflame with the Word of God. Carol knows her authority in Christ and has taught many of the rest of us to, also. She has a governmental anointing and has prayed prayers that shape the Nation.

The word of God is not just ink on a page. It is supernatural, alive with power, to regenerate, restore, heal, and recreate. Psalm 149:6 compares words of praise as having a two-edged sword in your hand. Hebrews 4:12 says, "For the word of God is quick and powerful and sharper than any two-edged sword, piercing even to the dividing asunder of soul and spirit; and of the joints and marrow; and is a discerner of the thoughts and intents of the heart. So if you are wanting to do some self-examining, just saturate yourself in the Word. The anointing and life in it will bring things to life in you.

Our tongue, like a sword, is powerful and useful. It can be our weapon of defense. In my mid-twenties I worked an office job in the computer room of a Potato Chip Factory. (The first place I ever tasted chocolate covered potato chips!)

One unusual evening leaving the office, I walked to my car alone. I had worked over a bit, which was unusual for me, so most of the others were gone. As I crossed the street a man appeared walking down the sidewalk. He began following me up the narrow parking lot which was between two buildings. The Holy Spirit placed an urgency to get quickly in my car.

I picked up the pace and got in only to have the gentlemen grab my car door and stop me from closing it. He began to give me instructions as to what was going to take place; but my tongue seemed to move without even thinking. I put both hands on the door and said very loud and forcefully, "In the name of Jesus!" and I did not even have to finish with, "I shut this door." Because the fear of God came over him and my door came shut and he was sprinting away as fast as he could run! I know he must have seen a warring angel with sword in hand because he was shaking in his boots! Whatever he saw I don't know for sure, but I know fear came all over him at the name of JESUS. The Word Jesus!! The sword is powerful. God placed a flaming sword at the Tree of Life in Eden to protect it. I believe that flaming sword is His spoken word. Genesis 3:24

To be able to speak is a beautiful gift. Not everyone on earth can even use his or her voice, you know. But to use one's voice to enhance the Kingdom of God; to speak God's Word, is the greatest privilege of all. It is not something we can even do without "supernatural empowerment". After all, it is from Him (Jesus). And since we are "in Christ" it is through the Spirit of Christ we speak. And all we do is as unto the Lord.

So, it is from Him, through Him, and to Him. All glory belongs to God for anything good that comes forth out of us. Every day is another chance to bless God and others. I, personally, am so thankful that His mercies are new every morning. For I am still not claiming to have attained perfection by any stretch, in the tongue area.

But Wow! ...I have seen the power of the miraculous when using the Sword of the Word and God's Will. You must believe in His heart of love, and His character, that He is a Good Good Father, just like the song.

2 MY SWORD, MY PROVISION

As we entered the new year there was a lot of prophecies regarding this being the year of the sword, according to the Hebrew Calendar. Now I do not speak Hebrew but Jesus was Jewish so I believe He used the Hebrew calendar and knew the Greek and Hebrew alphabet. The numbers and letters all have meaning. Thus, the sword represented by the Hebraic numbers 2017.

As the Hebrew New Year came, I would enter an area and the clouds in front and above me would reform and make the shape of a sword. This happened three times. God began to show me that this year the sword (the tongue) would be used as His Sword for the delivery of God's word. He also showed me he would use it to bring provision for me. How and when we open our mouths to use our tongue creates prosperity or poverty. This is regarding not just finances but provision and prosperity of spirit, mind, soul, and body. Prosperity is a state of mind and spirit where you know that God is going to provide.

One month we had an unusually high power bill at Life Streams. I knew we were going to be short of funds at the time. We had only been open a few months. Then faith arose in my heart and I lifted that power bill straight up in the air before my Abba Daddy God. I said, "Father, I am your daughter. And this is your ministry, so that makes this your power bill. I am just sayin' God, I know you are a God who pays your bills!". Of course my Abba

Daddy God came through! Within thirty hours, a call came and a major shipping company began renting the parking lot between the hours of 11:oo p.m. and 4:30 a.m. (a time we don't use it) for a whopping $1,000.00 per month.

Prosperity is knowing God cares so much for you that He will provide everything you need, spirit, mind, soul and body. That means relationships, too. Sometimes it's not on our time schedule but that stretches our faith and brings real break-through, too. To know God personally can sustain us in our point of need is a powerful shift. He knows what we need far greater than we do.

We can use our sword to speak things into the now! Too many times we pray as if we expect things "someday." No! We need to call it into the NOW! Believe and picture it in your head.

One hot day last summer's end I was driving across the lake near my home. I saw families hooking their boats together and having family fun. There were many boats zooming around the lake on the perfect sunny hot day. I said to God, "Why can't I have a boat?" I really want a boat. All of a sudden I heard a voice come back to me in the spirit, "Why not you?" I fired up my sword agreeing quickly and spoke out loud, "Why not me?" in faith. If God loves me- there's no reason I shouldn't have one!

One hour and forty minutes later as I was in my home preparing supper, I received a call; A dear Christian lady I had known for years was on the line and said, "Would you like to have a boat?"

Now my brain had shifted to earthly cares of the day and I quickly explained to her that purchasing a boat was not in our budget right now. Really, no matter how cheap, at that time we just couldn't fit one more thing in the budget! She calmly asked if I still loved going boating. I said, "Oh yes, in fact I was just talking to God about this a little while ago." That's when it hit me that there might be a connection with this and that! I got quiet. (I put my sword in my sheath.) She then said, "I have a boat and I want to give it to you!"

I questioned back with a statement as if to clarify, "You are going to give me a boat." She said, "Yes. It was given to us and we just aren't boaters." Now, I am hesitant to say, I was really a skeptic. I asked again, "You are going to give me a boat?" Again, she said, "Yes." Now I began to be amazed. God was just waiting for me to ask and believe.

That boat is now named, "The Miracle." This year will be my first year to use it as we got it at the end of summer last year and only had it out once. But, I declare, people are going to get saved on that boat, healed on that boat, and I will celebrate the goodness of God on it!! God is amazing me on a regular basis as I believe in His miraculous ways and use my sword for good.

My Sword, My Tongue

3 OUR SWORD CARVES OUR RELATIONSHIPS

"Whosoever keepeth thy tongue- keepeth the soul,"
Proverbs 21:23.

We shape our whole life by our tongue. We draw people close. Sometimes we repel people away by the fruit of our tongue. I once was sharing with a friend the effects of some people in life who had a sharp tongue and used to rip and tear with words. I could tell that they didn't really believe me about the extent to which people caused damage even though I gave some examples to which they gasped. They still seemed to think surely I exaggerated.

I shot up a prayer and asked the Spirit to make them understand. About that time a massive turkey- vulture came right down in front of the car we were driving. We both saw it and nothing further was said; I knew God revealed a visual aid for us both! I know it's dramatic…but God relates with me that way. The enemy can use ignorant and unlearned people to behave like a vulture picking, stealing, ripping, and tearing.

We need to realize it is the enemy behind it. De-personalize it and understand it is not the person, it is the enemy of your soul. It is the opposite of Life building. They are death words. Forgive them! Because the day will come someday when we will realize we have wounded someone by our cutting sword. And we must show mercy and forgiveness believing we will receive mercy when we need it. I have known that feeling too many times. Don't want to be there.

Until they get victory over that area proceed with caution. Proverbs 4:23 says guard your heart, for out of it flow the issues of life. Be careful what you share and how wide you open your heart. If it is really bad, you may need to avoid open-hearted, vulnerable contact with them. Limit the way and the extent of your connection. Proverbs is referring to exactly that when it says to guard. And you may have to put up a verbal stop sign a time or two. We all want to bring Life with the tongue. Holding back your tongue keeps your soul.

You tongue draws people to you or tears down relationships with others. We think we can take the liberty to cut loose on others with a sharp or critical tongue, but walls begin to go up in their hearts. If continually done day after day- you will wake up to find people pulling farther and farther away. And whether we realize it or not- we all need advocates and loving soul ties in this life of tribulation. Remember the wicked stepmother in the movie Ever After? She could find no advocate. Nobody wants to be her, lol.

On the other hand, people who sow good seeds of love with their words are planting beautiful trees of protection for themselves! Those are people whom understand the value of good covenant relationships. Loving family and friends sow back to you as God prompts them to… Just when you need it the most!! To tear down would be a picture of foolishness at its finest.

I pray for you right now that God gives you a new dimension of His wisdom in relationship building with the sword of your tongue. May you have a shift in that area that takes you into enhanced covenant relationships. God is a covenant God. He designed marriage and other relationships. He praises faithfulness throughout the Scriptures. Surely He is the most faithful of all. So Never Never see Him as eager to let go of you. He is a keeper of His own Words.

We bless with words not for selfish reasons- but out of obedience. Proverbs 21:23: Keep your tongue- keep your life from troubles. Proverbs 39:1: Sin not with thy tongue. But we are commanded to love others as ourselves. So don't forget to love yourselves enough to allow good relationships. No more self-sabotaging by cutting off those loving relationships when they mess up and hurt you. Say daily, "I Forgive all, and I choose life!"

We must let God Judge others' hearts. There is an office, the Apostle that is gifted to judge the fruit and actions of individuals in the church. They bring wisdom and even correction based on deeds; but never to condemn the person. The end goal is so that person will repent and draw close to God and be saved. Even the correction and reproof of the Apostle is in hope of repentence and restoration. Some times someone has to use the sword of truth before the light bulb comes on they have done wrong.

We all have authority over spirits. The Bible says we have been given all authority. We are seated with Christ in Heavenly places. We once had a vagabond came in to sleep in our motorhome parked on one of our properties. I keeping sensing a vagabond spirit. My grandson, only 7, said when he was in there he, "just didn't feel special anymore." I prayed a cleansing prayer and took authority over anything not of Christ. (I had destroyed the bedding, disinfected, purchased a brand-new Queen-size mattress which had to be cut to fit- $$). But only after I prayed was all good.

I will never forget the rejection and isolation we felt for that lonely vagabond. We prayed and used our sword to take authority over his life, binding an orphan spirit and a vagabond spirit to be removed from the gentleman, whoever he was and wherever he was. We never saw him, again. We believe he was reunited with his circle of influence.

We have liberty over an orphan spirit because The Word says we are adopted. Ephesians 1:5 says that we are adopted according to the good pleasure of His will! So use your sword to declare that every day! Thank You God that I am YOURS!

Maybe you have never started your journey with the Lord Jesus. It is as easy as 1,2,3

Believe in your heart that He is the Savior.
Not just that He is in title. Even the devil knows that,
but accept His payment for your sins.
His payment is good for all and
He promised you a Robe of Right Standing.

Thank Him for His forgiveness and salvation.

You are in!!!

Now tell someone, just to seal it in faith,

and date it here._____

Welcome Home, You are adopted.

4 MY SWORD, THE TONGUE OF REPROOF

"As an earring of gold or an ornament of fine gold is a wise reprover upon an obedient ear," Proverbs 25:12.

The Sword of Our Tongue is a helpful tool in reproving. I used to be a stickler about only speaking "feel good" words. I based it off of the New Testament verse that all prophecy should comfort, edify, and exhort. However, I failed to see at that time that to exhort is to call one higher.

And as much as I look forward to encouraging, and focus on that 95% of the time; God is showing me that there are benefits from reproof. When we keep the attitude that no human has ALL of the light - we know we all hold room for more. It is a form of Grace in itself. If no one ever told you that you had erred…You might have stayed in all kinds of darkness. As mature sons and daughters God is looking for those who are correctable and teachable. This usually comes through relationships. We can trust and allow those close to us to reprove gently. It should always be done in love. Love will be felt and received when done properly.

So, bring it on!

There was a time when God was downloading so much revelation and power everything I spoke happened. It even scared me at times! The Lord gave me a scripture ahead of time that people would fear me. However, He gave me instruction that it was in His plan and that He was clothing me, so to relax and trust Him in it all. During that time, it was as if He opened a flood-gate and reproof came from nearly every direction.

A huge variety of people gave instructional words and directions of reproof. I did NOT like it. It did not feel pleasant to the emotions. However, looking back over that season, I really was given powerful keys that unlocked things in the long running scheme of things. Since then I have altered my boundaries for what I am willing to receive and deliver regarding using scriptures of reproof. I have chosen to use the Word and let it do it's perfect work.

I found myself getting to a place where I actually say things to others asking for correction. Only those I truly respect and trust do I open that door to. I hunger for it. After all, the doors open earlier for you if you learn things earlier, rather than later! So now, when God leads I am willing to give a LOVING word or reproof.

5 MY SWORD IN THE SHEATH

Every good solider knows when to put his (or her) Sword in the Sheath! We speak life, we speak provision, but sometimes the Holy Spirit says silence!

When He does, it always pays off, I cannot stress this enough! The book of James says taming the tongue is the hardest thing in the world and that No man can do it! James 3:8: Only by the power (Dunamis Acts 1:8) of the Holy Spirit can it be done. A force greater than mere man.

The beauty of it all is that the Love Dove lives in us. He is here inside and just waiting for us to release His Love and Power to do whatever is needed to further the Kingdom of our Abba Father. Remember His Spirit at conception of our new walk became joined with ours. We can sense His will now and be in agreement with Him. Then the power (Dunamis) comes when we are speaking His desires.

So, we can let Him rule and reign and defeat the anger or pain that tries to bring the sword out when it needs to stay sheathed.

I read a women's book once regarding this subject and the lady said it was so hard for her- she had to literally close her teeth together on her tongue and hold it for ten seconds to pray silently and then the Holy Spirit would take over.

My Sword, My Tongue

I was once told that what we say "No" to, determines what we get to say "Yes" to! I have found this so true in my life! The more I have said "no" to my own satisfaction of getting my two cents worth in - the more and more and more God has opened doors allowing me to say "Yes" to wonderful opportunities that were far greater than I ever imagined.

I was once offered an unbelievable position in a well-known cosmetic company which would have come with amazing perks! I have always loved the art of cosmetics and making women feel good about themselves. It is an opportunity to speak into their spirit and walk them into the greatest step in the world, communion and intimate relationship with Jesus. He will meet them where they are, take them by the hand, and escort them into His Kingdom of Love.

This job offer seemed like a no-brainer at first glance. Any woman would love it. However, as I discussed it deeper with the Lord I felt a "no." Everyone around me (except a few) told me I was crazy if I didn't take it. It was a tough decision I didn't make quickly. I prayed for direction and guidance. After a lot of soul-searching I knew I had to put that sword in its sheath. Within two weeks, doors began to open for me involving Impartation, Commissioning, and Ordination. Then more opportunities to new doors of sharing the Gospel.

I knew I had made the right choice. God told me he would provide all I need. God brought supernatural provision which required no manual or physical labor on my part. I exhort you to say no to opportunities that are less than optimal.

When I was a mother of three small children I applied only for jobs that would allow me to get my kids off to school and be there after school. I remember one gal said to me, "Lady, you are never going to get what you are asking for!" I chose to keep my sword in the sheath until I was out of the building; but at the front steps I used it well. I said, "I rebuke that hopelessness and Lord I believe you will CREATE the perfect job for me if there is not out there!" Shortly after that I accepted a white glove job logging all the activity on their jets at a billion-dollar business that feeds the nations of the world. And guess what? It was through their temp-service so I could let them know what hours I was available. Bam! God moved again!

God causes us to triumph! Just as His people want their kids to be victorious, so does He. And He has the power to make it happen! The keys are the words we speak. THE LIFE YOU ARE LIVING TO DAY, YOU HAVE CREATED BY YOUR MOUTH! And knowing when to sheath your sword is eminent!! Sometimes what we DON'T say paints the clearest pictures!

A dear mentor friend of mine, Anita Mason, taught me well on many things. One lesson that stands out is one that she displayed as well as she spoke:

A bruised reed God does not want us to break and a smoking flax not to quench. God reveals in Isaiah 42:3 that he shall bring forth judgement unto truth. The Loving God that He is – Only He is worthy to judge the heart of a man. And He must be the one to handle it in His way and His time. I watched Anita show amazing supernatural grace over the last thirty-four years, to hundreds, maybe thousands of people. Even words of reproof and correction can be dripping with the honey of God's Love.

But to not snuff out a smoldering wick, sometimes means we have to hold back our sword with a force that feels like a team of twelve dark horses are at the other end of our reins.

Sometimes our sword doesn't feel dripping with honey- we feel like we want to chop, slice, and dice. This is a time when we must remember about a bruised reed and a smoking flax. Hurting people are the ones that hurt people. You were hurting once. We may have to take a time out and excuse ourselves to a quiet place to rein it in. Go to the ladies room for a time out. Pray in the Spirit until you get peace. The grace you extend will come back to you someday pressed down, shaken together, and running over.

My Sword, My Tongue

6 MY SWORD, MY TONGUE IN OBEDIENCE

I can't stress enough how important obedience is. We all have our humanity, of course. And its God given, so he understands it. Our sword still shapes our lives by what we speak into existence.

I was asked to attend a Franklin Graham planning meeting just before he was scheduled to come to the Illinois State Capitol. It was getting close to election time in 2016 and President Obama had just came and spoke.

The invitation came when I was feeling overworked and utterly exhausted.

The Pastor and his wife contacted me the day of the meeting offering free dinner tickets and even a ride to the Capital City. This was a very sweet invitation and we always have a great time when we're with this couple.

Everything in my flesh was screaming "No," from fatigue, but I was feeling the Holy Love Dove say, "Do it for me!" I remembered my husband was in St. Louis, MO and it would be tough for him to get there on time. I told them I would check with him and if he could make it, we would attend.

I phoned my husband, almost hoping he would say no. But, I prayed and asked God to let His will come forth. I spoke it out as a declaration feeling the sword release the fire. "I declare God's will WILL BE DONE ON EARTH AS IT IS IN HEAVEN-OVER THIS THING!" I spoke out loud with the sword, my tongue.

My husband isn't fond of business meetings, at least most of them, so normally he would have said no. As we chatted and I explained the invitation, he quickly agreed. I used the sword in my mouth to agree to go, out of obedience, feeling by now that God definitely was up to something! I felt such affirmation from the Holy Spirit that he was pleased. I asked God to give me His strength and He did.

The evening turned out to be very pleasurable with a lot of friends and colleagues there. To my delight, as the evening progressed, the Pastor who invited me turned and explained that he was needing a replacement to pray over the session of the Illinois Senate in one week. How honored I felt when he asked me to do this in his place.

The course of the day flashed through my mind. I knew God had gotten me there for such a time as this. I thanked Him for the opportunity and said yes. As I was introduced by the Speaker of the House and stepped up on the platform one week later, I knew "I was born for this moment."

What if I had not been obedient? What if I had allowed my tongue to be under the influence of fatigue instead of the sword of the Holy Spirit.

God woke me up night after night and told me what to say. He even showed me an open vision of Angels looking like SWAT Team members dropped down on ropes and stood by each person in the room as they got silent and looked directly at me.

God had told me to write the prayer out. This was a stretch for me because I had always felt like prayer came more under the flow of the Holy Spirit if I just let it come naturally. I was so glad that I was obedient and wrote it out because Illinois' Kingdom Congress asked to print the prayer in their newsletter, and I had it in written form to share.

When I refer to obedience I am not referring to the letter of the law. I am saying be obedient to what the Holy Spirit speaks to you to do. James 2:12 talks about the Spirit of the law of Liberty. Obey what the flaming sword of the Holy Spirit says to you which will always line up with the scriptures.

To hear this, you must know His Character. God is Love. He is not an angry God. He is not mad all the time. He is your loving Abba Daddy God. His mercies are new every morning. God is very smart! He is a genius at the details and always has your best interest in mind. If he is giving direction, He has something good up his sleeve!

You never know what wonderful things God has in store for you!... So always find a way to be obedient.

My Sword, My Tongue

7 MY SWORD ~ HIS REWARD

Everything good that I use my tongue and my voice to do… the Glory all belongs to Jesus! A friend once said to me, "It's Him!... from Him, through Him, to Him. This is because His wisdom is what does the miracles. Not our earthly wisdom but the Wisdom of Christ which brings new revelation and light that leaves one forever changed. (Read James)

So, it's from Christ, our Beloved! Then I am in Christ and he is in me- so truly I am a conduit or pipeline of Christ. All the good in me is really flowing through the Christ in me. Flowing through His free gift of righteousness…(Romans 5:17)… for we wear his robe of righteousness!! (Isaiah 61:10)

I delight greatly in the Lord; My soul rejoices in my God. For He hath clothed me with garments of Salvation, and arrayed me in a robe of His Righteousness!...

Then, we must do it all as unto the Lord, not for mere men. For some will be crazy about you (for a bit) and at other times people will turn on you like an ugly on an ape! So if it's only done for them you'll find yourself discouraged or disappointed!

However, if you do all that you do for Christ- no matter what happens here on earth; it was for Christ's reward, anyway.

Our successes and crowning moments we lay at His feet; for His Reward. We do it all because He first died for us.

8 MY SWORD, THE HARVEST SICKLE

The most important thing you will ever do with your tongue is lead people to the Lord. It is actually a transfer of kingdoms. Love comes rolling off your lips like sweet honey filled with light to those who long to go from darkness to Light.

Can you imagine what God the Father sees? I saw with the eyes of my spirit; laser-type light shooting out from a tongue with Golden Rays, when sharing the Gospel. I have actually had incidents where people cover their eyes at me when I came close to them in a meeting, arms up over the face, who have been in such grave darkness and depravity…such as witchcraft of black despair.

Hungry lives are out there every day seeking for a drop of kindness. We live in a world that can leave us cynical and guarded- but we are entering the most critical time EVER to release the Love of Jesus to those hungry for it. The day is at hand. No more delay! You will recognize them. They are the ones who stand out! They are angry, hateful, abandoned, hurting, and have walls up. But that is when our Sword of Love stands out the most.

My husband and I visited a massive Christian light display in another city years ago. As we drove through, the Holy Spirit, whom I like to call the "Love Dove," spoke to me and said, "…Notice how the lights show up so well tonight?" The night was as black as a chalkboard. The moon was hidden by the black clouds. He revealed to me…the darker the dark- the brighter and more beautiful the light.

In the dark and difficult times, the light will shine, shine, shine! It sticks out very noticeably in the dark! So don't be afraid to use that lighted Sword of yours! It pierces through the walls people have erected. It gets them to open up to you so you can reach them.

The harvest fields are everywhere! They are all around you; eyes watching, ears listening for you. Recently I walked into an upscale department store in our town. I was left a voicemail to pick up a gift with purchase item. As I arrived and revealed my name, the sales clerk began to squeal with excitement. She told me that she was really moved by my voicemail message. She said she was so touched that she had all her friends call and listen to it. She apologized for hang ups, saying that they had all called to hear my voicemail message.

My tongue and lips were used to pointing the way to Jesus in a simple, loving message. Easy… Steps 1, 2, and 3 on my voicemail. I was AMAZED how many people have called my voicemail to listen and left me messages saying how they are blessed. I had one voicemail that several called each day for a while when they first heard it. It was changing them.

I call it a "Harvest Tool." Facebook and hash-tagging messages are another amazing way to reach the world, also. My Sword- My mouth speaks of the light and truth into "Talk-Texting" and into a Facebook message- with a hashtag so lots of others can partake of it. Don't let your sword sit and rust in the sheath. In one of the recent Christian movies there was a man who had a dream he was in a wheat filled with a sickle. I have had that very dream. My daughter also had a similar dream. Every day God opens opportunities to use your sword as a harvest sickle.

I have seen the flaming fire of God move in miraculous power at the Sword of the Lord on the Tongue. Yet, I know the bankruptcy of my own words when it's just me or my flesh talking.

The Harvest fields are white. People are starving for the light. You have life in you.

      The value of intimacy with Him is so the key. Be alive, be in tune, be in Him, as He is in you. Speak Life. Speak Love. Every day you are speaking something into existence. Why not make it something beautiful unto Him and into His creation.

Prayer

Oh Father, I surrender my tongue to your flaming sword. May it be your beauty that flows through me and off my tongue, my sword. Set me on your path that I might glorify you.

My Sword, My Tongue

ABOUT THE AUTHOR

Debra Bettis Holt operates in the gift of Prophetic Exhortation. She is Commissioned in the Apostolic Anointing and is the Founder of Life Streams Center. She has traveled to Poland, Germany and El Salvador speaking and singing the Gospel.

She has been married 39 years to David Holt and they have three grown children and six grandchildren. She is Certified through the American Association of Christian Counselors in Biblical Counseling. She has attended Richland Community College and Oral Roberts University in studies of Communication. You may contact Pastor Douglas Lowery who served as her Pastor for many years at Maranatha Assembly of God in Decatur, Il.

She has served on the Heartland Apostolic Prayer Network at the Illinois State Capitol and been privileged to be introduced by the Speaker of the House to Pray over the Illinois Senate.

Debra Bettis Holt may be reached by:

Phone: 1-217-454-6200

Facebook

Email: Hartsong777@aol.com

Mail:
Life Streams Ministries
1681 N. 22nd St
Decatur, Il.   62526

Other books by Debra are forthcoming!

Author Photograph credit: Abigail Holt Allen

www.ingramcontent.com/pod-product-compliance
Lightning Source LLC
Chambersburg PA
CBHW070752050426
42449CB00010B/2436